Phantompains

Phantom

POEMS

pains

THERESE ESTACION

Book*hug Press
Toronto 2021

FIRST EDITION

Library and Archives Canada Cataloguing in Publication
Title: Phantompains / Therese Estacion.
Names: Estacion, Therese, 1983– author.
Description: Poems. | Text in English; includes some text in Visayan.
Identifiers: Canadiana (print) 20210105895 |
Canadiana (ebook) 20210106271
    ISBN 9781771666862 (softcover) | ISBN 9781771666879 (EPUB)
    ISBN 9781771666886 (PDF) | ISBN 9781771666893 (Kindle)
Classification: LCC PS8609.S73 P53 2021 | DDC C811/.6–dc23

PRINTED IN CANADA

The production of this book was made possible through the generous assistance of the Canada Council for the Arts and the Ontario Arts Council. Book*hug Press also acknowledges the support of the Government of Canada through the Canada Book Fund and the Government of Ontario through the Ontario Book Publishing Tax Credit and the Ontario Book Fund.

Cover artwork by Marigold Santos: *shroud in threadbare light 1* (detail), 2020, acrylic on canvas, courtesy of the artist
Design and typesetting: Lind Design
Type: Mundo Serif, Tungsten and Trade Gothic Next LT

Book*hug Press acknowledges that the land on which we operate is the traditional territory of many nations, including the Mississaugas of the Credit, the Anishnabeg, the Chippewa, the Haudenosaunee and the Wendat peoples. We recognize the enduring presence of many diverse First Nations, Inuit and Métis peoples and are grateful for the opportunity to meet and work on this territory.

Book*hug Press

To my parents—Jose and Maria Theresa

To my sister—Ann

To Ipo—Olivia

To L—Ezra

She is too raw to be cooked
—Herminia Meñez

As uncomfortable as vomiting is,
it can be very instructive
—Deng Ming-Dao

Contents

*

Once upon a time the spectacle   A young woman flatlined herself into oblivion   Seemingly so   Really she became the subject   A body made machine-dependent, tube down her throat her holes sliced and closed   lines for the drip taped to her skin   Organ removed   Her body was dead dying then automatic pilot   One time they brushed her tender gums so hard her mouth bled

Another time they would not let her speak to her mother father sister anyone   Apparently she needed sleep   Still she forced herself to stay awake   afraid she would never wake up again—   Awakened Nightmare Syndrome   Later someone asked how she was feeling   When she replied *psychologically perturbed* they took a syringe from the locked box and squeezed fluids down her neck forcing her to rest for tomorrow when they will sit her up for the first time   After all she does is sit stare blankly at walls the blurs and the clocks   11:30 turned into 12:34 into 1:41   twenty seconds past 3 a.m.   *When is lunch coming*   Oh gawd she was bored   At least they found a way to put her bed by the window so she could stare at a tree and someone once washed her greasy hair braided it beautifully for sleep   But let us fast-forward a little past the sanitary purgatory to a time when our woman-child would cycle in and out post-coma necrosis exposed mummified fingers and feet

A spectacle outside a spectacle   A beast that wore her dead hide outdoors

*

On a bed that moves, on a white sheet   *I may*
be over or under   Someone in the distance speaks
to me and asks my permission   *I guess*   Then, I
am in an elevator   Four people are around me

     Who are they?   I am wearing clothes, *mine or*
the hospital's   I cannot tell the difference   A
man with a coffee, a woman with scrubs

     I want to kiss them all
               They can read my mind

I am in another room   They say it will only
take three hours, or was it three minutes   I look up
and see large blades on the ceiling   They are
circling and circling, taking scans of my body

     Suddenly I am under bright lights   Someone is
telling me to look at the X-rays

  "Do you see this?   This?   It must be
done"   *I don't understand*

                              I nod   agreeing to it all

"Take deep breaths   Count backwards from five"

5,4,3 ... beep, beep, bee— A pause in time
Someone thinks that it is slipping away so they
work faster   Pump harder   I can no longer

feel   I am under bright lights again and on steel

      Cold   *Who else has been on this*
table?   *Were they able to wake up?*

A woman with a mask and rubber gloves strokes
my hair   Soundless

                                                      "Work is
to be done   Sleep"

                          An abrupt slumber   *Co m e   h e r e*
N o   N ot   t here   O ve r   t here

                                          Two figures are
waiting   They listen for my answer but there is no
question   I do not have words   I feel that I do not
want to move   I want to stay

      There
here
                  Here
         I open my eyelids   My parents' faces

                                          My face

I want to see my face

*

There were no goodbyes, no casket,
no kiss,

no sobbing   no epigraphs   no kneeling

just doctors in disposable masks and gloves—
that go in the same garbage can—

   my body   *belonging to my body for years*
go into—

          trash in a trash can—
   my body—trash—   trash

belonging in the dump—with their trash

   my body—flesh made trash   —theirs
to

         trash
  —garbaged body—   waste

Waste body   garbaged
     while I was anaesthetically asleep

naked under medical fluorescence

—intubated —dead bits cut off

        —dead bits deemed

"biohazard": waste

——~~feet~~

——~~ankles~~

——~~fingers~~

——~~Uterus~~

———~~biohazardbodyparts~~

all go into their fucking garbage can

Abat/Monsters

a rare bug caught, fusobacterium necrophorum
perhaps it was always in me, dormant, still

Agta

Ganahan man gyud ko namaka kita ku ug agta I've always
wanted to see an agta, the smoke ogre that lives in green mango
trees   They say that an agta used to live in the old tree
found on my ang kong Tyrone's front yard   Ni ingon sad sila
nakakita siya ug agta They said that he had seen an agta when
he was young

Di man ka makakita ug agta You can't see an agta *He* is the one
that chooses to see *you*   I'm not sure how this is decided   It
may be based on his fetish for naïveté or how bored he is that
day   Pero ni ingon sila na ang manga agta, beware, kay
But, they said that when you see an agta beware basig e
temptado ka nila ug paglaum because he will try to tempt you
with an offer you can't refuse: a wish

Morality is of no concern to agtas, so you need not worry if
you are a little shit   But be *careful*   He should never be
trusted   For instance, you might take up his offer and wish
for 100 million pesos so you can get into the cockfighting
business, breed prize cocks and win some matches that leave
the other rooster bloody,   perfect for sabaw soup

Later, the agta may decide to fuck with you   All of a sudden
your cocks are dead because your yaya accidentally fed them
raw beans

Now, you are old   Have no teeth,   no rice

Pero, sa bata pa ko, dili gyud ko kahibalo ani!

But, when I was a child, I had no idea!
I wished I could see an agta, eye to eye

And when katong na matay ko sa I died in August
I swear I saw something like an agta   At the foot of my
hospital bed   a form with no eyes

He said to all the devils that came

Ayaw Pag Ari Do not come here

Ayaw Pag Hilabot Do not touch

Duwende

Duwendes are little flat-nosed gnomes that
are known to be some of the first inhabitants
of the islands   They usually live sa gamay na bontod, og
sa sud, ug sa luyo sa inside hills, and mounds   Duwendes
are so light-footed that you'd never hear one walk across your
room

According to my tita, there are three types of duwendes: itom,
puti ug puwa   black, white, and red   All you need to know is
that a red duwende is ambivalent about you   A red one can
either fill your life with goodness or rot it with dread

Once, when my dentist was picking at my cavity,
she told me a story that a friend of a friend of hers told
her   *Apparently*, na-ay usa na puwa na duwende naka
sud diri   Apparently, a red one had been able to enter
This red duwende had fallen in love with her friend's friend and
had decided to latch on to her

The thought of a red duwende being here, possibly hiding
behind our bags of rice freaked the shit out of me

I was so afraid that I threw out every red object I owned
I hate red duwendes   I hate that my life has become a red
duwende

                Will I be okay?   I want to know

18

Afloat

Gi ingnan ko sa ako-ang pa pa na na-ay ukoy My papa told me
that there was a merman nag puyo dapit sa dagat who lived by
the sea in his hometown of Gihulngan   This merman and his
family lived there for years as fishermen

My papa told me that hibalo siya na ukoy sila kay baho kaayo
siya na buwad, he knew he was a merman because he smelt
so badly like fried dried salt fish, had green skin and webbed
fingers and toes   Papa said he once saw him dive into the
water from his boat, hunting sa dagat in the sea for days
When he finally emerged, he had a string of dalupapa giant
squid hanging from his neck

I think about this merman often when I'm sitting in my
prosthetist's office without my legs on   Seeing my limbs halved
without feet makes me wonder if I am a fish-person as well

Maybe somewhere down my blood line a perverted lola had
fantastic sex with an ukoy   Or maybe they did what they
used to do to their unwanted girls—dumped them in the water

Perhaps I was always meant to be the child who had to pay
debt to all their libidinal bestiality and female infanticide
An offering of my soles for their souls

Tianak

You may hear the cry of a tianak baby vampire while walking
alone at night by the rice fields or cemetery on the islands

The tianak uses its desperate wail to seduce any sense of
goodness you may have into cradling it   When you inevitably
succumb, the tianak will then transform into its truest form—a
red-eyed vampiric baby   One of satan's little darlings

        Iyahang change, mas pas pas gyud sya sa kidlat!
His change is faster than lightning!   Mu budlat iyahang
mata og mo dako iyang pupils...   His eyes enlarge and
pupils widen parihas gyud ug ka dako sa meaty tamarind seed
to the same size as a meaty tamarind seed   Dayon, Then
the tianak will thrust its fangs into your neck ug kanun gyud ka
niya! and he'd fucking eat you!

Hadlok gyud ko aning estoryaha sa una ... pero   I've always
been afraid of this story, for good reason But now, that I am
barren and without my uterus, I wonder if I may just decide to
walk the rice fields and cemeteries alone sa gabi-i para maka
kita ko ug   at night so I can find a anak para nako   child for
myself, even if it is satan's cherubic spawn

The White Lady of the Philippines

There was one type of ghost that repeatedly appeared when my friends and I told each other ghost stories during recess The White Lady—a woman's ghost who liked to float around schools, hospitals, cemeteries, and old homes

She looks like this:
taas ka-ayo iyahang buhok ug itom her hair is very long and black   Iyahang mata Her eyes ... usahay pula, usahay itom, ... sometimes red, sometimes black, uahay wala siyay eyes sometimes she doesn't have eyes   Dead eyes

We used to swap stories of various White Lady sightings while sitting on the grass waiting for the recess bell to ring   One time, a White Lady turned the whole kindergarten yard upside down para mu baliktad ang langit so she could inverse the sky Meanwhile, another White Lady roamed our hall's bathroom, feeling nostalgic about her school-ruler abortion   And once, during a nap, naka kita gyud ko ug I honestly saw a White Lady ... Nara siya sa kwarto ni mami ug ni papa na-ko ug iyahang kong gi tutukan ... She was in my parents' room and she was staring at me Pula gyud iyahang mata! She had fucking red eyes!   I immediately shut my eyes and burrowed between my parents, trying to convince myself that she wasn't really there

White Ladies can't actually *do* anything to harm you   They're just *there*   Wa silay kalibutan They're a bit clueless Sigi rana sila ug appearing and All they do is disappear in and out of rooms passively or melodramatically   Unlike these spectres, ni balik man ko I came back

Maybe with a purpose?   I don't know

Usahay, though, mu bisita siya nako   Sometimes, though,
she visits me ug mag higda siya tupad nako ug mag hilak and
lies down beside me and cries Kusog gyud iyahang hilak kay
makakita man siya She weeps and weeps and weeps. She
weeps because she can see our dead uterus lying sadly on a
pillow—mura gyud ug pagod na tocino looking very much like
the burnt pork belly at breakfast no one wants to touch

Aswang

An aswang is a type of abat that eats flesh
Aswangs are found all across the islands and vary in form and
personality   One story of a known female
                 aswang in Cebu goes like this

Sexy by day, at night she moves any way she pleases
Sometimes, she ends up at the disco where she laughs, mag
sayaw sayaw siya ug mag hubog   dances and gets drunk   She
laughs and pretends she is interested in your cock. Excuses
herself. Leaves. Finds a hiding spot. Dismembers. Hides her
legs by the garbage.   Grows fangs and wings becomes
hideous (but keeps her *perky* tits) ug mag huwat siya sa atop
and she waits for you perched on the roof

Pag lakaw na nimo, When you leave, that's when she gets you
           Hunt. Swoop. Crunch and glug. Dayon Then
                 she puts herself back together again, *FULL,*
Trapohan niya ang iyang totoy. Cleans her tits
                                          Struts home

There *is* one way to catch her, though...
      if you had the courage
This aswang has never figured out what to do
with her intestines.   So, if you ever find yourself
walking out at night and see a long, moist chord
swaying in the dark   *RUN*

Pero ako, ako siyang atangan kay But I, I wait longingly for her
I wish...   I wish I *was* her
        I wish I could put back together my dismembered body
Snapping my bones inside, tucking in my loose muscles and
nerves   Folding in my fangs & wings and sulod sa akong
lawas, daghana gyud ug sundang inside my body, thousands
of knives

I wish

        to be like her,
the whore butcher with a swinging rectum

Blood and Absence Flows

2.9 people out of a million
only 20 percent of us survive
septic shock
pelvic inflammatory disease
hysterectomy
necrosis
leg amputations
hand amputations
33 years old

Ancho

Misua angel hair noodle soup extinct,
soup language lost

Ancho used to serve
    her misua soup for breakfast
and wait for everyone
    to come into
the kitchen
    after a whole morning's worth of
her favourite pastime: laundry

No one knows how to make
    her misua anymore
The perfectly stern
      broth died with her
    Orderliness died with her
Stories of Ang Kong Vito died with her

I didn't know this at the time, but
    a future without our
siestas under her mosquito net
      on her thin, mattress-less bed with banig
        was arriving soon

I did not know this at the time, but
      seven years would tunnel
    my life before
      we could go back home,

before I saw her again,
     saw her strong laundry-hanging arms, hear her
talk shit in Amoy about her relatives,
        yelling "hao shao" or bullshit!

Before I could ask her what life was
               like after he left her
      and their children
      choosing the afterlife instead

When I finally came home,
    I saw her first
       Small, old, thin
limp in a wheelchair

why is her shirt so big?
why is she
      mute?

I saw her sitting in a rocking chair

      My dying nebula *ancho*
My spinning atomic
    single-mother matriarch in decay

ancho?
ka ila ka na ko? do you know who I am?

She saw me for a second,
    barely a second
and then

blank

Lady of Sorrows

Lady de la Rosa, black cloak caked crackled skin. All
year long she is hidden in my ama and ang kong's
home with all the other saints. Vision-questing in the
dark, speaking to pictures of the dead. Ang kong
Vito, the first to go. His black-and-white photo never
explains why he chose to die *that* way. I offer my
new sewage to them all. We lead the Good Friday
procession. Jesus Christ, we feel pain. Mother of
Mercy, Mother of Perpetual Help   *Come now*
                she says to us—moving mortared virgin.
             We step out with her. Blood and absence flows

Ama&Apo

We stuffed ourselves fat
Green mango&bagu-ong
   chicharon&rice
friedbanana friedcamote friedbanana
                          again   fat

   Fat,   fat stuffed, ready for siesta
Fat folding into each other
                Into fat arms, fat thighs,
   fat knees

Fat ama & fat apo
      Squeezing next to one another in
   the hot church pew
         Ama's fat arms fanning the heat away
with a py py,
                Apo leaning her head onto
         Ama's soft, lardy shoulders, cooling

Two fat round bibingkas
   freshly unwrapped from banana leaves

   Perfect
Perfect before siesta   during and
         after siesta

When mama came to pick me up
     after summer was over
          to bring me back to Cebu,
   she did not recognize my fat-chinned face

      I was fifteen pounds of
   Chinese chorizo and
        rice every day for merienda
overweight   *fat*

Me and you, we were *tambok*
     Tambokikoy

     Fat
sweet,
    When I finally came home

When I finally came home
    all your fat had worn away
you were
      fatless,   fatless arms
        fatless thighs   fatless knees

     made sullen by constricting
   parched skins   a confusing mouth

You are gone, *gone*   and what is left?

Our diasporic heartache

Smoke Struck

the energy of the birch tree burns
cranberry season in Denendeh

three women arrive
with joy and fish and an axe

i sit by the fire missing home
everything turns grey

my body rises
hanging with banana leaves

i am a puso/rice pouch from the islands
discarded sleeves opened

a salt crab crawls
stale rice shifts inside me

Tito Joey

delicately asleep in his coffin delicately tended to
each bead of his rosary delicately rubbed the
bruised skin on his forehead from rough repetitive
banging delicately swinging me on the hammock
delicately showing me a dead body for the first time
(delicately his own) circling delicately the indent
on the same banged spot on the wall in the solarium
with the pattern of a bull's eye   we would
fast-handle Hail Marys together with my mother
Hail Marys clicking against each other like a busy
staple gun
HailMary full of GraceHailMary full of Grace
HailMaryfullofgraceHailMaryfullofgrace
fullofgrace ofgrace fullofgrace ofgrace fullofgrace
Hail Mary full ofgraceofgraceofgrace
a brain filled with wind chimes

Elegy for Ang Kong

On the balcony
we sat together

Another long pause is coming
you take off your jade

        Remember me when I die?
Don't say that, Ang kong
will be back

*

I have come home to mourn
your humid plot in the cemetery

To sit in your room, on your
shrinking bed

While a praying mantis comes
to look at me, all verve

*

Papa says it was you
passing the bamboo trees

At dawn, I get a sundang
and hack all the green stalks
piece by piece

Staying Present

And when vomiting happens, it happens mightily
It is forceful and complete

—*Everyday Tao*

I vomited once
on a speedboat with my family

My mom and sister in the cabins,
me and my dad on deck

The crossing from big island to
small island was too balod for everyone

Clenched cranium, heaving chest, flexed throat glands,
dislodged tongue
I resisted the urge to hurl

Puke yellow pandesal,
sour orange Tang left my throat in chunks

> *You will feel better now*
> *We're almost there*

The horizon was still far away
I hate enduring

Got Sick

*body was once strong and capable, a machine
body regressed, state of infancy*

Pee

1.

I placed my coffee cup on the roof of your
car   Before that we had stopped for a sandwich
and I tried peeing   but could not   Two days
          before my failed attempt   the doctor at t
he walk-in clinic
            made me pee in a cup   I waited and then
another doctor read the results and said it was a UTI
                        He asked if I had
                                any allergies, I said
            penicillin   he wrote it down   went
to the back   came back with antibiotics and
            took the bottle

        We went back to the car   I took a pill

waited and struggled to stay awake on the
                                ferry ride back
        My body felt like
                    moss

2.

The night before the walk-in clinic   we slept in
            your friend's musky van   It was
cluttered with mementos
            like lint and torment   I wondered
when he last washed the   sleeping bags and

how often he had sex there
           I thought of calling the ambulance that night
                           but our bodies
were full of drugs   I did not want to bother
    anyone and get in trouble   I felt good
                       but
underneath the drugs   pain

       Who knew it was a big deal

3.

Earlier that night we partied   took our dose
cramped his boat's cabin
                 and danced between
the rusty furnace and newspaper piles

         ingesting
          the night

The boat stayed steady as we steamed
           Sooty windows nicotine
        Feral energy dripped on our bodies

  There's a picture of the four of us cozying up
after dancing   our heads jammed close to the cabin's roof
    the deck was empty   the light bulbs

      screwed tight   Our eyes

       apart

4.

After the boat   the van   the walk-in clinic   the ferry
the first pit stop

we stopped at a blue motel for the night   my body
                                                    felt cold
but my belly felt pain

                    Muscles gnawed away at one another

        I went to the bathroom   I wanted
needed to pee   badly

                        I sat for a while   Nothing came

Is the medicine working?

5.

The next day   you packed up our things and I
went straight to the car
                    I fell asleep
                        You drove   drove
    drove some more and finally stopped at a
                        coffee shop   I forced myself
to get out of the car and use the bathroom

                        Nothing came out
except a small trickle of blood

You waited outside the bathroom and
handed me coffee or maybe I lined up and got a coffee ...
I don't remember ... all I remember clearly:

I placed my coffee cup up on the roof of the car,
I looked at you and said   *I'm peeing blood*

                                                                Now?

                                                 No, when I was on the toilet?

I closed my eyes
                                         Something's wrong

The ambulance
     your car

                         Terror is in control now

You remember everything   this is your part to tell
                                     to feel

I wish I could take this part away from you

6.

Your terror not mine   I   instead held my
breath holding my belly

moving through   *here*
                                    N o   N ot   t here   O ve r   t here

7.

Here,   life   in a millisecond
                              showed itself

            and my body was flown from Trail, BC
and through
            the Okanagan thermals

                        I imagine that the sound of the
helicopter blades
                  dragged my soul
            back to   my sick body

                  bloodless battered   body   while you sped,

chain-smoking across the land without stops or
                                                            sleep

8.

You called my parents to let them know
their daughter was dying   to pick up my body
    say goodbye

I'm sorry you had to feel that
I want to go back, right here, to say I love you

9.

Somehow   plans changed and I survived the
night   You called them again to tell them to go
straight to Kelowna Gen.   So they flew from ON to
                        BC   praying and
rushing   praying and praying and praying

10.

With divine permission,   your presence

my decaying body went through repairs:

    a tube for urine,
    another one for poo,
    a machine for my kidneys
        a drip for the fentanyl, other opioids,   and food
    a vacuum seal for the incision down my stomach
            a tube for my lungs
        lines and machines with buttons

doctors and nurses working over

time

and on the 7th day of trial and error

I finally peed

11.

I woke up and you were gone,
        gone to sort out your job, to be able to
come back and forth to visit me

                    Here

                    I open my eyelids
My parents' faces
        Hi ma, hi pa

                            Can you
wiggle your toes for us? That's good, Inday

sleep

                    , stay

12.

You came back a week later   I wanted to ask
        I didn't know what to ask   I
couldn't ask   I was intubated   catheterized
      attached to many
             lines   machines   and
     loopy

13.

             You saw my pee   golden
liquid flowing through my catheter and into the
        pee bag   a sign of life

  You lifted the bag up to help my pee drain
from the catheter into the bag and smiled

         You smiled at me
                    I saw my pee
for the first time

     I   move

14.

   Thank you, Ez, always
My love, always

Iron Body

I am no longer attached to my flesh.   Even so,
it is difficult to go out into the world like this
Half other   I am sometimes afraid of the
hurtling   Our assigned junkyards filled with
medical equipment and assisted-living devices
My body moves in prone mode exposing some
truth stored in our limbic systems   Perhaps
I am a heroine in the iron mud

Coma Dreams

I should have stayed in my coma
Screaming is silent in a coma

Everything is so hard
My mind, my memory, my life

My body,
no longer whole

I should have stayed in that coma
Why did you wake me?

Death is possible

Hands

I am dreaming of what my hands once
were   Not the bulbous and scarred ones
I have now   My left looks like a sock
puppet My right has four mini Vienna
sausage fingers stuck to a palm that is
perpetually open   I do have
one thumbnail left   Once a month,
she demands 20 minutes of my time to
groom I have to soften her in lukewarm
water first before I chop off her ridges I
paint her in pastels so that she doesn't
alarm others   I never really dream of my
new guillotined hands   In my dreams, a
pair of complete hands, alien to me, show
up instead   I have no clue whose hands
they are   The fingers are shorter and
hairier   The nails are too round   The
cuticles brittle and gnawed   No   The
hands in my dreams are not *my* hands
My hands are, or were, perfect, slender,
refined   Far from ever looking like
canned hotdogs   When I wake
up, I try to recall what the bastards were
doing that night   What were they
tearing mercilessly?

I cannot control hands that are not mine

The Amputee by the Magnolia Tree

I am a lump of gas sitting
by the hospital's magnolia tree

A geriatric smell surrounds
me in the infirmary

I am too young to be old
Too odd to be young

Amputations bloom
my name fades

The ABG (Able-Bodied Gaze)

Itwatches   *alwayswatches*
It walks behind me in the park and proceeds
to walk slowly to get a good look   *It*
follows&follows&follows   *&watches&watches*
&watches   I turn around   and
    Itlooksaway   I begin to walk as
quickly as I can   gaining some speed but
Itfindsme I stop *Itstops* I walk slowly again
Itwalksslowlybehindmeagain   Finally I
turn around to say: HELLO   but
Itpretends I'm inconsequential that I am
being paranoid   *It* was just minding its own
business all along
    Why am I bothering *It?*
My mistake

    Itlooks up at the sun feeling absolved
Ityawns   *It'sbored* of me already

Report on Phantompains

I

Phantompains are a type of pain you feel
even though your limbs are no longer
there For instance, you may feel a quick
electric shock like an unravelling lightning
bolt that shoots up your residual limb
Sometimes it feels like your arteries have
been caught in subcutaneous mousetraps

II

There are some phantompains that
register higher on the phantompain
threshold   Three days after my bandages
were roughly removed by the resident
assigned to look after my limbs I felt
the beginning of insurmountable pain re:
electric shocks   But I did not say anything
to him I never knew how bad it could
get   No one prepared me

III

On the ambulance ride to the rehab
hospital   the pain worsened   Every time
the paramedic drove over a speed bump
or pothole a sharp blade jabbed into my
phantom ankle

IV

I arrived at the rehab hospital late Friday
afternoon   It was the weekend and
the amputee unit was quiet   All of the
main staff were off along with the unit's
designated physician   The doctor on call
gave me 200 mg of gabapentin to start   It
was not enough   It takes 2 days for the
body to absorb the dosage given   No more
than   200 mg can be given and it has to
be given every 2nd day to give the body a
chance to absorb the drugs   Small daily
increases were never enough for my pain

The limit: 800 mg

What I needed that day: 600 mg

What I was on: 200 mg

V

For 3 days my ankles felt like they were
being nailed to a cross, even though they
were already gone   The pain always
became worse when some of the nurses
forced me to go on the commode despite
my requests for a bedpan   They said
that this was good practice but really
I think they were eager to see me get
better   The pain was always worse
after physiotherapy   It felt like a huge
boulder was brought down like a hammer
on my "ankles" over and over and over   I
couldn't breathe into the pain   All I
could do was contort during the moments
when the pain felt like I was being crucified
(I imagine) The physiotherapist tried an
electroshock machine on my residual
limbs aka stumps   It didn't work

VI

My family looked on   The nurses
looked on   The doctors worried a vein
had ruptured   They all looked guilty
and inept   I needed to focus on the pain
and not on their tortured faces   No one
was allowed to touch me and they finally
stopped forcing me to go to physiotherapy

and let me use the bedpan   A nurse
brought me a chocolate bar since she felt
sorry for me   My doctor prescribed
the most beautiful drug in the world:
nortriptyline

VII

Day 5 was better: 600 mg of gabapentin
2 Gravol a day plus sweet nerve-numbing
nortriptyline   I was only allowed to be on
nortriptyline for a week

VIII

There is a difference between phantompain
and phantomsensation

IX

Phantomsensations—feels like my nerves
are buzzing, similar to your vocal chords
when you hum   My legs are constantly
saying *hmmmmmmm hmmmm*   The
humming never ceases   I just try not to
think about it   The buzzingbuzzingzzzzz
keeps me company where my feet cannot
I can feel them now

X

There are also non-physical phantompains
many amputees feel   Some of which
include: hyper-vigilance,   paranoia,
melancholia, PTSD, violence, futility,
extreme loneliness, detachment   No two
phantompains are ever exactly the same

Recommendation for further inquiry:

The phantomfuture: I just can't help
wondering what it might be like for me as I
age and become more fragile   Will I be
able to carry the weight of my prosthetics,
let alone put them on?   Silicone liners,
socks, sleeve ... they share a combined
weight of 8 pounds   That's 4 pounds
per leg   It doesn't seem like much, but
with a crumbling knee and saggy hip joint
at seventy or even sixty that may turn into
a shit show

The pain of knowing that the hospital
bed might be my permanent future
someday soon is something that I try to
compartmentalize alone at night   alone
loneliness and sorrow hustling in front of
me   alone   my heart cramping up
like a charley horse

ICU I

the trachea
    leaves
my throat
      like steel wool

i swallow
once and demand   w a t e r   &

                solid food
                ~~any~~ food

    they force me to wait   to drink
and am only
      allowed to eat
        crushed ice

Tony   my nurse
        gives in and feeds me
    crushed orange pops

everyone is mad that I am mad

        no drinking   *no liquids*   no *satisfaction*

    my tonsils
corrode

rust
    spreads

inside

ICU II

i am
    floating Jell-O

dizzy
        gelatinous
                pancake
with a wobbling cranium

a big baby
        with a
jellied neck

    i practise
sitting up

first
    in a wheelchair with a headrest
                my head swinging like
                        loose molecules

    time to practise
sitting up:

                10 min. today
            twice that much tomorrow: no
                    headrest

but the nurse forgets about time
and eats her lunch

my jelly neck stays up for
23 minutes or one
thousand
three hundred eighty
seconds

i almost become vomit

resisting being
a jellied woman

mopped up

ICU III

i arrive
        at a laughable five seconds
    late
      like a damaged
    cuckoo clock

        new and
bizarre baby
        reading
            their lips
      for the punch
line
          offering them
beige eyes
          that slowly make
                            their
              way down
          past

wormholes

                  and
            old wood
    that
          rots

      the

                sun

A Task

there was no use in being afraid
surgery was inevitable
I was always meant to undertake

Thinking about things again:
misery during leg amputations month

something is wrong
my body
erred

/ outside

good morning,
a new smell from your necrotic feet

I sit up and see
　　　　my dead foot
　　　　separating from my ankle

　　　　　　an oblong hole
　　　　　　　　exposing
　　　　　　　　　　dry
　　　　　　　　stiff tendon
holding together my
　　　　mummified left foot

one dirty gas station jerky tendon
　　　　　　holding it all

my nurse explains

don't you *want*   /   *get it over*
with
start your *life*   /
post-surgery recovery room:

   my calves amputated
skin wraps around new
residue of limbs

tightening
         bruises tighten and tighten

    It hurts

   the nurse hears the third time
     It hurts ,hurts
/stitched sawed bones

       /muscles   / panic /
nerve endings/   panic
       panic
       panic

   she widens the spout
   drugs begin to race

the bruises   /   cool

I /

    static/

after

the first
  /implosion

               morphine mimics
                  and mimics and lies to

                  block   pain

          underneath
                sheath is truth /

          a whole universe
                  reacts *still*

          into a box   / I

                      boom

no room in the hospital to cry

/at night

I strangle

/bite my cheeks/

on tonight's
  "grief schedule"

y o u
  w i l l
b e

  losing *your* shit

in the hospital everything
        is rhythmic

I am wiped every day,

        every day rhythmic
after every bedpan mishap/

I know
outside the bubble of medical
fantasia

I will be left
alone/

  /choosing
meds   all by

        myself/

        to stop

fake day walking sham

    what's really left
over is plugged
carbon fibre socket
limbs

  a residue

/
gambling with

what's left

perhaps   all
hysterectomies are an
emergency mine kept
me alive the gyno says
good thing · *you won't*
have uterine cancer

great. one less organ
in my body revolting
against me

  /I
walk home

   under
moonlight/   cratered

        /sinking
dust
    bowls
              it is true

   some voids are

/   pointless/

Eunuched Female

something new,
cycle

EF I

2 days after de-intubation   Sister finally
confesses:

                                 The bacteria attacked your reproductive
organs, they had to do   *a hysterectomy*
Eunuched Female says: *Why are the walls upside down?*   Sister
continues: *They had to take out everything,*   *even the crib*
Eunuched Female thinks of a mirror   She needs to see her
vagina now   Instead Sister was forced to cement: *Your eggs*
were all black   Eunuched Female feels vacuous
    How long was she holding on to that fact for?   Her sealed
abdomen loosens

There isn't any hysteria, just thoughts   Like: *Does my vagina*
still work?

Eunuched Female tests out sex in post-surgery ward 4 weeks
after hysterectomy   She asks Lover:

                                   Stick your fingers in
                                        Please

He worries her neighbour will wake up   worries he will make
her more ill   *Please*   *just put it in*
He obliges   Stealthy sex with malady on floor 8 ensues
Includes:

_spoiled gauzy hospital panties
_night nurse interrupting to
    check blood pressure
_L drops his belt buckle loudly
_Mrs. Brown suspicious of lover being
    there past 10 p.m.
_moaning behind the cheap unwashed
    curtain
_humping around an IV drip
_quickie

Lover gets nervous   Eunuched Female whispers: *Just cum inside please*   He does and this eases her eases him

Eunuched Female is still paranoid her vagina is ruined   She wants to do it one more time just to be sure

Eunuched Female cannot help it   Melancholy throbs below the hole   So, L will have to oblige her more than once

While somewhere outside her window,
the crooked pine tree
hatches her an anvil

EF II

Waiting for her amputations   Eunuched Female calls
Lover, who has left again for the mountains   L calls
every night except for Thursday   On Thursday he parties
Eunuched Female doesn't care   *cares*
There are other things to worry about

Two dates:
a. leg amputations
b. hand amputations

Her holes are never aroused anymore since she has been
infantilized by

_everyone who sees her

It's not their fault she *is* in a motorized totally unsexy wheelchair
that has only 2 speeds: worm or slug   both asexual beings
like her

At least her dead feet are gone   Instead she has **stumps**
Engorged scabby stumps that need to be trained to withstand
extreme pain   and shape themselves slim   She is
instructed to wear liners coated with silicone

*They will help your **stumps** shrink so they can fit into your
prosthetics   Don't worry, they hurt to put on at first,   but
then it's just like putting on eyeglasses   You'll see*

Eunuched Female tries to wear her liners despite the pain   *You have to get used to the pain*   *You can't be fitted for prosthetics with swollen **stumps***

Every morning they come in the hospital room and check her **stumps**   Every morning they will look at **stumps** and say: *Your **stumps** are healing nicely*   Eunuched Female wants to scream   STOP fucking CALLING THEM THAT

Training her **stumps** hurts   Putting the liners on hurts and they squeeze her stitches: skin stitches   vein stitches muscle stitches   scabby stitches   Thank God for the drugs   She is given lots of drugs for pain that feels like crucifixion   Her favourite is nortriptyline   The first time she took the pills she felt like copulating gelatin   Sister phones her that night: *How's it going?*
Eunuched Female: *I can't talk right now I'm on drugs*   Sister laughs: *That good huh?*

Eunuched Female wonders if she can be on nortriptyline tomorrow   and   the   next   day   and   so   many   days after   Naturally she was only allowed to have it for a week   The other drugs were not as nice   They gave her vertigo and haze

During the day Eunuched Female works hard to keep her shit together   Keep her shit tightly together while exercising eating therapy-ing crying Keep her shit together while talking to God and smilesmilesmile   smile   Be rehab hospital's favourite little disabled darling   smiling at the public while rolling down the hall at slug speed

   Last thing she wants to do is complain   She wants to grow up   get out there   be sexy again with skinny **stumps** Be ready for Lover not be ashamed of fat gross drugged-up loser **stumps** and gross scabby leaky gangrened hands with scary hard blackened mummy fingertips and ugly iodine-stained fingernails

   The sooner she complies and smiles the sooner she can give everyone a boner again

stump—*cut down a tree*
stump—*saw a leg below or above knees*

But if you touch
if you caress your sawed leg
the sawed tree

matter beats

EF III

Lover finally visits on Christmas   2 months after

a. extreme nailing on the cross phantom pain
b. extreme confusion about who she is

4 days after Christmas they are finally alone and spoon on the futon in her parents' living room while everyone is asleep upstairs   Eunuched Female watches L's eyes to see where he looks   She tries to hide her stumps under the blanket but the weight hurts them   Don't worry, her liners are on
                                        Good girl

Eunuched Female tells Lover: *Be gentle*   Her hands are still necrotic   brittle   Her stumps are still babies   Her hair is still falling out   Lover enters her and she thinks of crying but doesn't   She decides to cum instead   *Good girl*

Fireworks pin the sky during NYE   L and Eunuched Female sit beside each other   She on her wheelchair and L on the futon   His hand is on her thigh   her limb on his   Lover is leaving soon   Soon she will be back in rehab preparing for surgery no. 2   He will call her every day again except for Thursday Eunuched Female will miss him and resume:

—wake up
—see falling hair see dandruff hair
—transfer from bed to wheelchair commode
—morning pee/bedpan pee

—face   pits   peehole   poohole   sponge wash
—hair brushed teeth brushed
—get ready for day in day pajamas
—look forward to rehab hospital's entertainment, i.e. Café
   Night Mondays   Cake&Coffee Tuesdays   Bingo Wednesday
   Ice Cream Thursdays   daily lunchtime vendors that sell
   things like costume jewellry   hand cream   silky scarves
   outside normalcy etc.
—look forward to daily visitations by family and friends
—look forward to/not look forward to/have to take meds
—800 mg of gabapentin
—Gravol
—stool softeners
—blood-thinner injection into belly
—no more nortriptyline
—absorb meds then slug speed straight to physio
—workout on h e a v y drugs
—lunch   nap   stare   socialize   *repeat*   *see below
—special days: psychotherapy/spiritual care   lose grip
   get a grip   lose   gets   loses   grips

———————— **Sample Day with gangrene fingers** ————————
post-leg surgery pre-hand surgery

—fingers are falling off
—gangrene pus skin oozes between good skin and hard mummy
   fingertips
—a new nurse is assigned every morning
—cleaning rotting fingers is tedious business most nurses avoid
—new nurse is often temporary nurse or on-call nurse
   unsuspecting nurse   clueless nurse

78

—Eunuched Female spends time training new nurse on how to clean and bandage: wear gloves + open kit + unwrap old pus-soaked bandages wrapped around each finger + throw away old bandages + *try not to comment   be horrified   pity patient   hold your breath   remember you   are the professional here* + pour saline solution in small basin + dip cotton balls + gently clean pus off with cotton balls + replace dirty cotton balls with clean ones + leave to air dry + cut 5 strips of iodine using shitty medical scissors into 1 inch W × 5 cm L + prepare small pieces of medical tape + peel clean iodine strips + lay iodine strips on clean surface + wrap iodine strips around gangrene pus-y smelly bleedy part + tape strips closed with prepared medical tape + make sure bandages are tight so they don't slide off + repeat for each finger and two thumbs+throw away gloves + wear new gloves to prepare tubular gauzes+cut tubular gauzes into 1½–2 inches + slide gauze delicately on top of each iodine strip wrapped fingers + clean up + *pat yourself on the back for learning a new and rare nursing skill*

—some nurses are faster   gentler   cleaner   kinder more thorough than others   best is when Sister does this on her visits   bestest is when Lover did this during her Christmas break
—EF feels disgusting the moment she wakes up
—She has felt this way ever since her fingers started to gangrene approx. 2 months
—2 months of belonging to rotting and oozing body parts
—also feels sorry   shitty   shitty to feel&know fingers are dying
—feels especially shitty when Mean Nurse is Today's nurse

—Mean Nurse often makes a face and holds her breath when cleaning fingers
—Mean Nurse has told EF and others that EF is "a lot of work"
—EF takes revenge dump on Mean Nurse whenever she can
—MN has to wipe Eunuched Female's freshly shat ass

---------------------**End of Sample**

repeat:

meds + parents fuss and care during daily visits + druggy physio + lunch + more meds + chug Ensure + prosthetic fitting + parents coo + parents socialize or do errands + EF slug speeds to chapel for alone time + cries secretly beside dark-skinned Mary who is holding sweet-faced baby Jesus + stare confusedly at White Viking Jesus with muscles and seductive eyes + stare at tree by window + nap + parents come back + parents stare at EF while she naps + post-nap grogginess + more meds + wait for friends to visit + "host" friends + bring friends to rehab night activity + slug speed in wheelchair to get best spot on Coffee&Cake night + hopes this week's performers are cool + EF thinks: *If they sing "You Are My Sunshine" again I will kill myself or kill them* + performers sing "Skinnamarink" to the institutionalized instead + EF: *ugh*   despite secretly loving the song + say goodbye to friends   goodbye to parents + get ready for bed + talk to L if it's not Thurs. + enjoy nightly cookie snack + enjoy night meds

_doesn't cry   doesn't cry

_*don't cry*

Member of Nice Nurse List sits with Eunuched Female one night and tells her she caught a couple having sex in the bathroom once

He was in the bath chair and she was straddling him, true story
EF: what did you do?

I closed the door and let them be

But tonight Eunuched Female thinks about hand surgery scheduled tomorrow and can't sleep   Today's night nurse is Mean Nurse   EF tells MN she's scared—   *scared*scared Mean Nurse doesn't care   Says   *Just don't think about it*

The door shuts,   *shuts*

groaning
in my insides

EF IV

Vaginal Dryness—a condition that afflicts most post-menopausal women and hysterectomied women   Purgatory is dry   Necrotic fingers above gangrene are dry   Post-rehab life is very dry   Eunuched Female used to confess about masturbating   She used to lie and say she was always dry   EF: *I am now disabled and dry   desperate*

Lover leave me: pursue warmer sex

Lover come back: I will prove I am still sticky

Gynecologist tells EF that   *It's not sexual to moisturize your vagina every day, besides the walls are looking pale, less fleshy Women in their 30s are supposed to get their "second wind"*   EF: Of course

Eunuched Female buys expensive organic lube and pours cups of it on her amputated hand   On the bottle it reads   *"To prevent mummification of vagina, pour daily"*   She rubs like a child

She wants to keep L and visit him wherever he is   Continue attempts at de-Eunuchization knowing there will be no miracle child

L   comes   and   goes   comes   again   again   goes again   goes and comes in the way one flosses a street dog's teeth for the first time

While he is absent   EF decides to take advantage of being
alone

Alone she closes a door open and touches her vagina   touches
and touches   &touches

Fries to sizzle

fries, fries

to sizzle

Hello?

EF V

It has been two years and Eunuched female can now do two very important things:

—wipe her own ass
—drive

Lover escapes again this time to North of 60 hoping to start anew   Eunuched Female follows him desperate for more than sex   He obliges unwillingly   *willingly* again   A hopeful adventure on taiga rock

The aurora is thick with green particles and they fight often Often they spoon   Often she is alone and waits and watches the fox burrow and travel across the ice road while he skis the pain away

When she feels like mould   she drives onto the frozen lake takes her dead uterus and places her in the passenger seat

Last night   L wondered again if it was his fault

Was it the dirty lube, the "butt stuff"?   No   *so don't stop making love*   she reminds him

A sun dog interrupts   and shines on her flaccid uterus
All 3 suns seem real and steady with heat   She pockets her
uterus and slowly walks to a part of the   freshly ploughed
ice   She peeks into the patch and tries to figure out how
deep the freeze reaches   The wind scrapes the fissured
flecked lake

Uterus says out loud:
   They said only 2.9 out of one million people get the bacteria

EF: Fusobacterium necrophorum?

Uterus: *No one knows where you got it from*
                   You're ... We are a miracle
                   Remember, remind L again

EF: Sure

Uterus: *Well, at least you don't want to kill*
                        yourself anymore

EF: That's even *more* tiring

At home   Lover calls her and asks what kind of chips she wants
and how much ricotta to buy for the lasagna   The birthday
card he gave   her sits on the table

It reads:

> *through*
> *wind*
> *and snow*

Outside   the light pushes past 5 p.m. again   Soon
the sun will begin to strong-arm the snow and stay

Eunuched Female holds Uterus up to the window and checks
for specks   A black raven interrupts them and flies
Something new   cycles

A rock waits for a billion years,
waits for them to arrive

gives them dreams

*

to do this again/   the plasma tunnel/   a vision /

                               my soul

                      a guard lights a cigar at the
edge of my bed   /he crosses his legs /
    filling in the edges   /   *agta?* / so, I decide to
finally rest with *him* by my side/

           was it the drugs?/I often mistrust my memories/
but I came back to this

sudden stops might be better/   instead,
                        industrious

                  closings   /

*

Walking on the butterfly path/   I've barely torn out

of my

            garbage bag coffin—innards barely back

together / *barely*

Grace attended my burial/   the windstorms
                              were unanimous

let her rise   :   a cripple,   bare

*

For my feet, for my fingers, for my Uterus

All I can offer is a memory

they were full
they were ecstatic
           & in flux

Resources/Sources

Explorations in Philippine Folklore by Herminia Meñez

Everyday Tao: Living with Balance and Harmony by Deng Ming-Dao

Earlier versions of some of the poems found in this book were published in *Contemporary Verse 2 (CV2)*, *Homesick Zine*, and *Pank Magazine*. I am thankful for the editors for giving my work a chance

The chapters' epigraphs were from a personal narrative I wrote for *EdgeYK* magazine. I am grateful for Laurie Sarkadi, who accepted my proposal to write my narrative and gave my work a soft place to land

Folktales/horror tales: all of the monsters or creatures were introduced to me as a child by various relatives and classmates when I lived in Cebu and visited Guihulngan (the Visayas). I am indebted to my Nanay Melba, who told me many of these stories whenever I asked her to

The Visayan written is a combination of the Visayan you would hear in Cebu (a city) and Guihulngan (a small town). The spelling of the words was verified by my Ipo, grand-aunt, Olivia Tiu

The idea for the first untitled poem came about after reading the first sections of Guy Debord's book *The Society of the Spectacle*

The idea for "Eunuched Female" was sparked by Germaine Greer's book *The Female Eunuch*

The poem "Aswang" became more comprehensive after reading Maximo D. Ramos's *The Aswang Complex in Filipino Folklore*

The cover art is a detail from Marigold Santos's *shroud in threadbare light (1)*. Her work is immense in both scale and meaning

Much of my book was written on the land of the Anishinabek, Huron-Wendat, Haudenosaunee, and Mississaugas of the Credit First Nation. A great portion of my book was completed on the land of the Yellowknives Dene, Samba K'e. The book's final preparations took place in Tiohtià:ke/Montreal. I hold an incredible amount of gratitude for the land and the Indigenous People of all these lands

Acknowledgements

This book would never have been written if it weren't for the surgeons and nurses who believed my life was worth saving. I wish with my whole heart that I could name them. I do not remember anything about that night in Kootney Boundary Regional Hospital, but it is certain that they saved my life.

I remember: Dr. Wilson, who made sure all my intestines were clean and healthy by checking every inch of it. Dr. Ng, who made the incredibly tough call of removing my reproductive organs, which has allowed me to continue creating. I will always remember your compassion. Dr. Ryan Foster, who took care of my delicate body and my delicate family, making sure that balance was eventually restored. Dr. Syed and his team, who stitched every little vein during my leg amputations and said I was his Mona Lisa. Dr. Anastakis and his team, who took care of my fingers and always made me feel like everything was going to be okay. Dr. Dhilkas, my physiatrist, who ensures that my legs can take me places with comfort and are in good health. Dr. Dhillon, West Park's amputee unit's doctor, who always made me feel like a human being , despite being a ward of the hospital. I hope you all understand that some of my angrier poems, regarding our medical system, were written from the base of my grief.

Thank you to the nurses and various staff at Kootenay Boundary Regional Hospital, Kelowna General Hospital, Toronto Western Hospital and West Park Healthcare Centre's amputee unit who cared for me. You all gave me the support and motivation I needed to bear the more dire parts of my stay in the hospital.

Thank you to my prosthetist Winfried Heim, who listens and cares. Please don't retire, ever. Thank you to my first spiritual care counsellor/psychotherapist, Steve Hudecki. The solace you provided made room for me to meet sacredness in a rather medicalized environment.

To my family—all my Titas & Titos, cousins—thank you for all of your prayers, visits, food, company, support, and love. Thank you to the Gallego and So families for helping my parents pack and move all of my belongings from my home so that I can one day move back. Thank you to all my cousins: Abing, Andoni, Anton & Rochelle, Bea & Nishant, Dominic & Chantal, Jayne & PJ, Jordan, Yumyum & Stef. Thank you to Jayne, Abing, and Yum Yum, who kept me company when I was housebound. You saved me from some lonely Friday and Saturday nights. To my cousin Emma: love forever. Thank you you to my Tita Agnes. I miss you and know you are here celebrating this achievement with me. Thank you for bringing joy and fun into our lives.

To my loyal and loving friends—both old and new. Thank you for your multiple late-night visits, love, and prayers. Thank you to Angie Ghandi, Gosia & Seb, Fayeanne & Jeff Spec, Kerith Paul, Khilan & Avionne, Kristina Alvaro, Laura Giovinazzo, Lyndsay Kane, Peggy & Jason, Riz & Ben, Zack, Alex Trica, Morgan Perabo, Jen & Josh.

So grateful for my Love Potion No. 9: Cat "Bonne Mama" Fournier-Bedard and Marie "into.her.light" Claude Michaud. Your love is a constant reminder of the gifts of friendship. Blessings and thank you to the Kinship, who continue to teach me about awe and reverence and flow: Hazel Courage Bell-Koski, Maria

Katherine Aksic, Shareen Shazeena Ally. All my love to Big Tree Crew: Jessica Udit, Maria Peters, Pam Gregorio, Vanessa Grandis. You are family. Thank you to Ania Trica—whose friendship and sisterhood I lean on.

To my St. Edmund Elementary crew of 2016: thank you for being more than just co-workers, and for your prayers and compassion. To Angela Abbatangelo, Andrew Nasato, Brian Ellison, Grainne Maddison, Helen Borrowitz, Joanne Roddy, Josephine Currie, Lisa Drost, Mary Ellen Gucciardi, Mdm Wolczek, Nuno Tomè, and "Momma Bear" Paula Smith: thank you for your mentorship and friendship. To Anna Maltby: thank you for fighting for me and making me feel like I belonged.

Thank you to the instructors I have had the pleasure to cross paths with at U of T's continuing studies' creative writing program. Thank you for your feedback, your instruction, and brilliance.

Much gratitude to Kirby aka, knifeforkbook, and Hoa Nguyen for providing space and guidance in your workshops. "Pee" and some parts of "Eunuched Female" came out during our study of Anne Carson's work Float.

Thank you to the Ontario Art's Council, and to Contemporary Verse 2 (CV2), Homesick Zine, and Pank Magazine.

Thank you to the NWTWriting society for your encouragement and feedback.

Thank you to Marigold Santos, whose cover art acts as this book's talisman and enticing invitation.

Much gratitude to India Amara. The roses you've adorned on my arms will continue to remind me of all matters of importance.

To my psychotherapist, Diana Orgera. Your practice saved my life. I am so grateful for your wisdom and compassion. Thank you immensely.

Thank you to Hazel Millar and Jay MillAr. The publishing of this book has allowed me to experience the other side of suffering—celebration. I am forever grateful for the opportunity you've both given me to share myself. Creativity thrives because of people like you and places like Book*hug.

Thank you to Tamara Faith Berger, whose yogic acuity and advice I rely on. Namaste.

Thank you to Marcie and Manny Black for always welcoming me into your home, and Sam and Adam, as well. Thank you for your generosity—the best food and wine—and the swimming at Lesage. Thank you from the bottom of my heart.

To Sara Peters, my first poetry instructor and editor. Your belief in my work still baffles me. I am so grateful for your friendship. Thank you.

To my editor, Brecken Hancock: my work has matured because of your generosity and encouragement. I could not have finished this book without your insight. Thank you for all you have taught me.

Thank you and love to my Ipo, Olivia Tiu, who understands me when no one else does, and my dog, Scooby, who is my angel.

Ezra Black: thank you for providing levity and tenderness when things were too bleak to withstand. I am lucky to have you in my life. I cosmic-love you.

To my sister Ann Estacion: I can never thank you enough. You are my anchor and life raft. I love you forever.

To ma and pa—Jose and Maria Theresa Estacion—who both, in my six-month stay in the hospital system, only missed one day of visitation due to a snowstorm: my life is blessed because of all the sacrifices you both have made for me. Ma—thank you for teaching me how to pray and love. Pa—thank you for teaching me the importance of discernment and patience. Your love is the reason why I am who I am. I love you both and hope to be able to take care of you the way you took care of me.

To my ancestors and the Divine Miracle: I am here only because you are here.

PHOTO: ANGELA GZOWSKI

About the Author

Therese Estacion is part of the Visayan diaspora community. She spent her childhood between Cebu and Gihulngan, two distinct islands found in the archipelago named by its colonizers as the Philippines, before she moved to Canada with her family when she was 10 years old. She is an elementary school teacher and is currently studying to be a psychotherapist. Therese is also a bilateral below knee and partial hands amputee, and identifies as a disabled person/person with a disability. Therese lives in Toronto. Her poems have been published in *CV2* and *PANK Magazine*, and shortlisted for the Marina Nemat Award. *Phantompains* is her first book.

Colophon

Manufactured as the first edition of
Phantompains
in the spring of 2021 by Book*hug Press

Edited for the press by Brecken Hancock
Copy edited by Shannon Whibbs
Design and typesetting by Lind Design

bookhugpress.ca